Why remember Philip Doddridge?

The life and labours of a faithful servant of Jesus Christ whose testimony provides inspiration in our challenging times.

BY ALAN C. CLIFFORD

CENTER *for* BAPTIST STUDIES
at THE SOUTHERN BAPTIST THEOLOGICAL SEMINARY

Why Remember Philip Doddridge?
© 2023 Alan C. Clifford

Published by: H&E Publishing, Peterborough, Ontario / The Andrew Fuller Center for Baptist Studies, Louisville, Kentucky

www.hesedandemet.com
www.andrewfullercenter.org

All rights reserved. This book or any portion thereof may not be reproduced or used in any manner whatsoever without the express written permission of the publisher except for the use of brief quotations in a book review.

Design and layout: Quinta Press (quintapress.com)

Paperback ISBN: 978-1-77484-133-4

eBook ISBN: 978-1-77484-134-1

First edition, 2023

Philip Doddridge

WHY REMEMBER PHILIP DODDRIDGE?

HE WAS MAN OF GOD

In brief, the age of Wesley, Whitefield and Edwards was also the age of London-born Philip Doddridge (1702–51). An utterly-committed albeit gracious Nonconformist in the great Puritan tradition, he was a pastor, preacher, theologian, apologist, academy tutor, author, hymn-writer, philanthropist and patriot. Indeed, he was a remarkable English Christian by any standard. His faithful, fragrant and far-reaching testimony to Christ made him unique in his day. He was a pioneer in the mighty revival and missionary movements which had a profound impact on UK and world history. He contributed to the Methodist Evangelical awakening which had a saving and sanctifying religious, social and political effect on 18th century society and beyond. It helped avert the kind of bloody revolution experienced in France in 1789.

That said, Philip Doddridge is usually remembered as a hymn-writer. For the majority of English speaking Christians, their knowledge of him stops there. This article is concerned to demonstrate that Doddridge represents all that is best and biblical in the 'evangelical Congregationalist' tradition. His evangelicalism is conspicuous in his hymns, and his convictions regarding church order and baptism place him in that denomination of Protestant Dissenters known as 'Congregationalists'.

As a hymn-writer, Philip Doddridge needs no introduction. The hymn books of many denominations suggest that his name will not be forgotten. 'Hark the glad sound' and 'O happy day' still find a place in worship of God's people. It is no small commendation that 'O God of Bethel' was chosen for the late Queen's Silver Jubilee service at St Paul's Cathedral in June 1977.

Yet Doddridge's hymns were just a fraction of his vast literary output[1] and an even smaller part of his many and widely creative activities. Apart from Doddridge's regular preaching ministry, the hymns might never have seen

---

1 See Erik Routley, 'The Hymns of Philip Doddridge', in *Philip Doddridge, His Contribution to English Religion*, ed. Geoffrey F. Nuttall (London: Independent Press, 1951), 46ff. Hereinafter *Doddridge and English Religion*. Also Ernest Payne, 'The Hymns of Philip Doddridge', in *Philip Doddridge*:

the light of day. They were written to supplement the sermon, and given out, line by line, after it had been preached. The hymns were used as a teaching aid, designed to reinforce and apply the preached word. This fact reminds us that Doddridge was primarily a minister of the Gospel of Jesus Christ, a calling which he considered 'the most desirable employment in the world'.[2]

From the time of his settlement in Northampton, in December 1729, to his death in October 1751, Philip Doddridge served the cause of Christ with intense energy and total dedication. As Charles Stanford wrote in 1880, he 'seemed to live so many lives at a time'.[3] In addition to being the pastor of Castle Hill Independent Church—his ordination took place on 19 March 1730—he was principal tutor of what was to become the most famous of all the Dissenting Academies.[4]

CHRISTIAN INTELLECTUAL

The dual role of pastor and tutor involved Doddridge in a wide range of interests and pursuits. As a tutor, he became an apologist (or defender of the faith), philosopher and a man of science, besides being a theologian, training young men for the ministry. What Doddridge managed to accomplish in 21 busy years was directed by a single preoccupation. In the words of Dr Geoffrey Nuttall, evangelism was 'the thread on which his multi-coloured life was strung. It was for this above all that he wrote, preached, corresponded and educated his students in the Academy'.[5]

Whereas a certain amount of interest in Doddridge has been generated in recent years, more attention has been paid to the man than to his beliefs. This is understandable, since Doddridge was an attractive personality by any standard. However, it is also unfortunate, since for Doddridge personally, his faith and his life were of a piece: what he *was*, was due, in great measure, to what he *believed* and *thought*. At least two reasons can explain the deficiencies in current Doddridge interest. *Firstly,* if Doddridge was not an original and profound thinker of the stature of Augustine, or Thomas Aquinas, of Luther, Calvin or Barth, he was an independent one. *Secondly,* since the mid-twentieth century, little interest has been shown in the kind of theological convictions shared by Doddridge and his generation (not least among the confessionally-correct advocates of John Owen's theology, suspicious of Doddridge's sympathies for Richard Baxter). This was stated

---

Nonconformity and Northampton, ed. R. L. Greenall (Leicester: University of Leicester, 1981), 15ff. Hereinafter Greenall.

2 Job Orton, *Memoir of the Life, Character and Writings of the late Rev. P Doddridge, DD of Northampton* (1766), in Doddridge, *Works,* ed. Williams and Parsons (Leeds: 1802–5), i. 260.

3 Charles Stanford, *Philip Doddridge* (London: Hodder & Stoughton, 1880), 41.

4 See Irene Parker, *The Dissenting Academics in England* (Cambridge: CUP, 1914), 101.

5 Introduction to *Calendar of the Correspondence of Philip Doddridge, DD (1702–51)* (London: HMSO, 1979), p. xxxv.

quite explicitly in the bicentenary celebrations of Doddridge's death in 1951, when Roger Thomas said, 'The important thing for us, however, is not Doddridge's theological opinions'.[6]

Renowned as Doddridge was for his gracious and charitable disposition, it has become necessary to dispel the myth that truth and conviction were unimportant to him. His daughter's oft quoted retort to a critic of her father's theological views, 'My father's orthodoxy is charity'[7] has reinforced the fact that, in his lifetime, Doddridge was accused of being indifferent to theological convictions. The truth, however, is otherwise, although in an ecumenical age, one is not surprised to find that the myth is preferred to the reality. Whilst Doddridge always lectured, preached and wrote according to the apostolic maxim of 'speaking the truth in love', it must never be forgotten that it was undiluted Biblical truth which he attempted to proclaim. We must not allow Doddridge's charm to seduce us into neglecting Doddridge's theology.

In acquainting his students with philosophy and scientific questions, Doddridge wanted them to be thoughtful preachers, who would be able to say *why*, as well as *what*, they believed. He believed Christianity was capable of a rational defence. He was therefore concerned with apologetics. Doddridge's reply to Dodwell's *Christianity not founded on argument* was his most ambitious intellectual piece of writing, in which he demonstrates that faith and reason do not necessarily conflict.[8]

Like the Apostle Paul in his debate with the Athenian philosophers, Doddridge wisely and graciously challenged the arrogance of the learned infidel, as a prelude to exhibiting the glorious Gospel of the God of Truth. Had he lived longer he would have engaged with Voltaire, David Hume and other anti-Christian sceptics. His lectures and other publications reveal a Christian mind, working out the philosophical implications of biblical truth. He was not intimidated by the secular 'Enlightenment' humanism then in vogue. As a rigorous evidence-driven biblical scholar, Doddridge demonstrated the total integrity of authentic Christianity. His apologetic would have no cause to fear the Darwinian threat of the next century. As a Christian intellectual, his efforts were foundational to a vital contribution to the spread of the Gospel during the great Evangelical awakening. Failing to recognise this, Colin Brown's book *Philosophy and the Christian Faith*, provides a highly doubtful assessment of the eighteenth-century evangelical scene:

> As with Luther, so with Wesley and the many who had similar experiences of God in the Evangelical Revival, this meant that the whole of life must be

---

6 Roger Thomas, 'Doddridge and Liberalism' in *Doddridge and English Religion*, 134.
7 Thomas, *Doddridge and English Religion*, 35.
8 Ibid. 469ff.

looked at in the light of this continued experience. The guide to life was the Word of God. Philosophy was set aside. There were more important things to do. No doubt this was true. All the same, it was a pity that no one in the Evangelical Revival attempted to work out the philosophical implications of their faith (a notable exception was Jonathan Edwards (1703–58) in America).[9]

But Jonathan Edwards of Northampton, New England was not the only exception. The Northampton of Old England could also claim to have a champion in the conflict between Orthodox Christianity and Enlightenment secularism. However, like Edwards, Doddridge was primarily a man of God, and he never lost sight of his goal. If Doddridge was seeking to provide a decidedly Christian education, his primary purpose was still to train men for the Christian ministry. We must never lose sight of the fact that this educator was a minister of the Gospel of Jesus Christ, and He was clear in his task:

> It is my heart's desire and prayer to God that not one (student) may go out from me without an understanding enlightened from above, a heart sanctified by Divine grace, quickened and warmed with love to a well-known JESUS, and tenderly concerned for the salvation of perishing souls. What are all our studies, labours and pursuits, to this?[10]

The task before us is to allow Doddridge the theologian to speak to us. It would have been much more *entertaining* to dwell upon the purely biographical and anecdotal details of this godly man's life, but we must be concerned, not so much with entertainment, as with instruction. My desire is to complete the picture, to correct any misconceptions, and to justify a continuing study of the life and work of Dr Philip Doddridge.

BIBLICAL BAXTERIAN APOLOGIST

What we are doing needs little justification. Serious Christian people are aware that important issues demand our attention. Since the appearance of John Hick's *The Myth of God Incarnate* (1977), multi-faith hostility to Christian distinctives has grown. Relativism has grown exponentially. It is also the day of pro-Chrislam ecumenism, with its negative impact on evangelism. Strident liberal theology, the Charismatic movement, Catholics and Evangelicals Together, and a host of other issues are part of the modern mix. The Christian Church is a restless institution, uncertain of its message, and doubtful of its relevance or place in the modern world.

Whilst Philip Doddridge is no infallible guide, he did at least address himself to issues very similar to those which face us today. Since these issues

---

9 C. Brown, *Philosophy and the Christian Faith* (Leicester: IVP, 1969), 80–1.
10 Ibid. 98.

are of eternal significance, we are not being retrogressive in considering some of his views, although they were uttered around 300 years ago.

Doddridge lived at a time when rationalism was gnawing at the roots of Christianity. Since fierce theological controversy was common-place, it was no easy thing for a young minister to be certain which opinion best reflected 'the mind of God in the Scriptures'. It was a day of extremes, and Doddridge believed with Richard Baxter before him that the Bible demanded a 'middle-way'. That meant avoiding the incipient fatalism of much High Calvinism on one hand, and the implicit humanism of Arian-Arminianism on the other.[11]

Contrary to my biography of Doddridge,[12] Dr Robert Strivens—while documenting areas of doctrinal agreement between the two men—seems anxious to distance Doddridge from Baxter as far as possible.[13] It was certainly never my concern to claim that Baxter was the only major influence in Doddridge's development, but an attempt to play down his influence indicates a nervous aversion for Baxter that Doddridge definitely did not share. When Dr Strivens concludes that Doddridge was 'in all the most important points, a Calvinist'[14]—an early statement from 1724 equally applicable to Baxter himself—he fails to appreciate the true significance of Doddridge's mature position. Indeed, in 1748, just three years before his death (the date only mentioned by Dr Strivens in a footnote), Doddridge unambiguously declared that 'Baxterian Calvinist' was 'a very proper expression'.[15] The point is not that Doddridge wasn't a Calvinist but that he wasn't an 'Owenite Calvinist'. Notwithstanding an appreciation for some of John Owen's books, this was obviously important to Doddridge regarding the nature and extent of the atonement and the nature of justifying faith (inclusive of obedience).

In his Academy lectures[16] we see how rigorous the intellectual training Doddridge provided for his students was. In his teaching method he was 'liberal' rather than 'dogmatic'; in other words he encouraged free enquiry. He was impatient with any theological system which failed to observe the balance of Biblical truth. Scripture was to be the only ultimate authority. He was concerned that truth itself, rather than his or any man's opinion, should mould his students' minds.

---

11 See Geoffrey F. Nuttall, *Richard Baxter and Philip Doddridge: A Study in Tradition* (London: Dr Williams's Library, 1951).

12 See Alan C. Clifford, *The Good Doctor: Philip Doddridge of Northampton—A Tercentenary Tribute* (Norwich: Charenton Reformed Publishing, 2002). Hereinafter *Good Doctor*.

13 See Robert Strivens, *Philip Doddridge and the Shaping of Evangelical Dissent* (Farnham, Surrey: Ashgate, 2015).

14 Ibid. 45.

15 Ibid. 24; see *Calendar of the Correspondence of Philip Doddridge, DD (1702–51)* (London: HMSO, 1979), 287; see also my *Good Doctor*, 137, 169 and 254ff.

16 See *Lectures on Pneumatology, Ethics and Divinity*, in Doddridge, *Works*, iv-v.

Doddridge's essentially conservative outlook is best seen in his *magnum opus*, *The Family Expositor*,[17] and his *Dissertation on the Inspiration of the New Testament*.[18] Reinforcing the fact that John Wesley acknowledged his debt to it in his own *Explanatory Notes upon the New Testament* (1754), the former excellent work justifies Dr R. Tudur Jones' observation that the author stands 'high amongst those who have helped people to understand their Bibles better'.[19] His theological foundations being assured, Doddridge was an advocate of the 'good old evangelical way of preaching'.[20]

METHODIST PIONEER

Nowhere is Doddridge's commitment to evangelism more clearly seen than in the welcome he extended to the infant Methodist movement.[21] Indeed, Doddridge's final decade brought him into close fellowship with the Methodist leaders, John and Charles Wesley and George Whitefield. His friendship with them and others, was typical of his spirit. When older Dissenters, including Isaac Watts, viewed the revival with cool and suspicious detachment, Doddridge was ready to perceive the hand of God at work. He rejoiced that God had raised up such men, in such an ungodly age. The new Dissent turned to the old for guidance. Responding to John Wesley's request, Doddridge provided a reading list for Wesley's preachers. After reading Doddridge's sermon *Christ's Invitation to Thirsty Souls* (1748), Whitefield wrote to the preacher: "... dear Sir, I must thank you for your sermon. It contains the very life of preaching, I mean sweet invitations to close with Christ. I do not wonder you are dubbed a Methodist on account of it."[22]

It is interesting to note that although this sermon was published in 1748, it was first preached soon after Doddridge settled at Northampton in 1729, six years before Whitefield's conversion and nine before John Wesley's. Doddridge wrote of the occasion that "something of a peculiar blessing seemed to attend the discourse, when delivered from the pulpit; and that to such a degree, as I do not know to have been equalled by any other sermon I ever preached."[23]

Here then was evangelical Methodism at Northampton, at a time when Oxford Methodism (in its 'legalistic' phase) was in its infancy. Thus Professor Alan Everitt has written: "If any event can be regarded as beginning the

---

17 Many editions were published. See Doddridge, *Works*, vi-x.
18 *Works*, iv. 168ff.
19 *Congregationalism in England* (London: Independent Press, 1962), 465.
20 Orton, in Doddridge, *Works*, i. 153.
21 See my 'Philip Doddridge and the Oxford Methodists' in *Proceedings of the Wesley Historical Society*, XLII. 3 (1979), 75-80. Also Alan Everitt, 'Philip Doddridge and the Evangelical Tradition' in Greenall, 31ff.
22 *Good Doctor*, 172.
23 Ibid.

Evangelical Movement it is probably the appointment of the Independent Philip Doddridge to Castle Hill Chapel in 1729."[24]

Furthermore, while Oxford Methodism was still 'legal' (or 'non-evangelical'), Doddridge was preaching a [Baxterian] 'Calvinistic Methodism' similar in character to the evangelistic theology of Whitefield. The style of the two preachers was also sufficiently similar for one of Doddridge's to pass as one of Whitefield's! When a selection of the latter's sermons was published, it included one entitled, *The Care of the Soul*.[25] In fact, it was preached by Philip Doddridge on June 22, 1735 at Maidwell in Northamptonshire![26]

Evidently, Doddridge the erudite academic was able to edify all and sundry. A humble ploughman from Weston Favell provides a glimpse of the impact of his regular pastoral ministry. During conversation in the fields with the then proud, self-righteous, unconverted Anglican Rector James Hervey (later a close friend of Doddridge and the eventual dedicatee of *Christ's Invitation*), the ploughman declared:

> You know I do not come to hear you preach, but go every Sunday with my family to hear Dr Doddridge at Northampton. We rise early in the morning, and have prayer before we set out, in which I find pleasure. Walking there and back I find pleasure. Under the sermon I find pleasure. When at the Lord's Table I find pleasure. We return, read a portion of Scripture, and go to prayer in the evening, and I find pleasure.[27]

Beside his hymns, Doddridge's own lasting contribution to the revival was his most popular book, *The Rise and Progress of Religion in the Soul* (1745). There was also a public political impact in all this. It was to the reading of this book that William Wilberforce the future anti-slavery campaigner traced his own spiritual awakening.[28] Consistent with this social aspect, of equal importance to Doddridge was the practical impact of the gospel. He was no armchair theologian. As co-founder of the Northampton Infirmary and promoter of a charity school in the town, Doddridge demonstrated the power of Christian example. His patriotic activity in connection with the invasion of Bonnie Prince Charlie in 1745, when he urged his congregation to join the Northampton Militia and thus helped to decide the invaders to turn back at Derby, reveals his sense of Christian social responsibility.[29]

---

24 Ibid.
25 See Revd George Whitefield, *The Care of the Soul Urged as the One Thing Needful* (Inheritance Publications, 1972) republished from *Sermons on Important Subjects by the Revd George Whitefield, AM* (1833).
26 *Works*, iii. 283ff.
27 John Whitecross, *The Shorter Catechism Illustrated* (London: The Banner of Truth Trust, 1968), 56.
28 See R. I. and S. Wilberforce, *The Life of William Wilberforce* (London: John Murray, 1838), i. 760.
29 See Malcolm Deacon, *Philip Doddridge of Northampton* (Northampton: Northamptonshire Libraries, 1980), 114ff, and also Victor A. Hatley, 'A Local Dimension: Philip Doddridge and Northampton Politics', in Greenall, 77ff.

As with Mozart in another context, one feels that Doddridge's life was cut short. He died and was buried in Lisbon, whither he had been sent by his congregation in the hope of restoring his health, at the age of 49. One cannot but be amazed at the consistent Christian dedication of a life all too brief. His life and example have bequeathed a rich and lasting legacy to the churches.

THEOLOGICAL CONVICTIONS

Despite his well-argued misgivings over confessional imposition, Doddridge was, pre-eminently, a biblical theologian in the Reformed tradition. He believed in the full Divine Inspiration and authority of the Bible. For him, the Bible was the Word of God. In his *Dissertation on the Inspiration of the New Testament*, he tackles the issues which still trouble biblical scholars. His view of inspiration does not lead him to deny that the human instruments employed their own choice of words; he is not therefore committed to the crudely mechanical dictation theory of inspiration. Whilst denying that the original documents had any errors, he does not feel that the cause of truth is lost in admitting the possibility of minor errors in copies. Doddridge emphasises the relationship between *inspiration* and *authority*:

> Nothing can be more evident, than that a firm and cordial belief of the inspiration of the sacred scripture is of the highest moment; not only to the edification and peace of the church, but in a great measure to its very existence. For if this be given up, the authority of the revelation is enervated (or weakened), and its use destroyed: The star which is to direct our course, is clouded; our compass is broke to pieces; and we are left to make the voyage of life in sad uncertainty, amidst a thousand rocks, and shelves, and quicksands.[30]

For Doddridge, the Bible itself is above theology. It tests and regulates our thinking:

> Let us therefore always remember that we are indispensably obliged to receive with calm and reverend submission all the dictates of scripture; to make it our oracle; and, in this respect, to set it at a due distance from all other writings whatsoever; as it is certain, there is no other book in the world, that can pretend to equal authority, and produce equal or comparable proofs to support such a pretention. Let us measure the truth of our own sentiments, or those of others, in the great things which scripture teaches, by their conformity to it. And O that the powerful charm of this blessed book might prevail to draw all that do sincerely regard it, into this centre of unity.[31]

---

30 *Dissertation on the New Testament, Works*, iv. 168.
31 Ibid. 193.

HYMNS

FOUNDED ON

VARIOUS TEXTS

IN THE

HOLY SCRIPTURES.

By the late Reverend
PHILIP DODDRIDGE, D.D.

Publifhed from the AUTHOR's Manufcript
By JOB ORTON.

I efteem Nepos *for his Faith and Diligence, his Comments on Scripture, and many Hymns, with which the Brethren are delighted.*
Eufeb. Eccl. Hift. L. 7. C. 24.

SALOP,
Printed by J. EDDOWES and J. COTTON:
And Sold by J. WAUGH and W. FENNER,
at the *Turk's Head* in *Lombard Street*;
and J. BUCKLAND, at the *Buck* in
Pater-nofter Row, LONDON.
M.DCC.LV.

CHRIST's Invitation to thirsty Souls.

A SERMON

Preached at

NORTHAMPTON,

in the YEAR 1729.

And now PUBLISHED

Chiefly for the Benefit of the POOR, at the earnest Request of a Gentleman of the Established Church of *England*.

By P. DODDRIDGE, D. D.

LONDON:

Printed and Sold by J. WAUGH, *at the* Turk's Head *in* Gracechurch-Street. M.DCC.XLVIII.

[*Price* Six-Pence.]

THE
Perspicuity *and* Solidity
OF THOSE
EVIDENCES
OF
CHRISTIANITY,
TO WHICH THE
Generality of its Professors among us may attain,

ILLUSTRATED and VINDICATED;

In a LETTER to the AUTHOR of a late Pamphlet, intitled, *Christianity not founded on Argument, &c.*

By P. DODDRIDGE, *D. D.*

WE *also believe, and therefore speak.* 2 Cor. iv. 13.
An High-way shall be there;—it shall be called THE WAY OF HOLINESS;—*the way-faring Men, tho' Fools, shall not err therein.* Isa. xxxv. 8.
Quis non contemplatione—concutitur ad requirendum quid intus in re sit? Quis non, ubi requisivit, accedit? ubi accessit, pati exoptat? *Tertull. Apolog. cap. ult.*

LONDON:
Printed for M. FENNER, at the *Turk's Head* in Grace-church-street; and J. HODGES, at the *Looking-Glass* over-against *St. Magnus* Church, *London-Bridge.*
MDCCXLII.

A COURSE OF LECTURES

On the PRINCIPAL SUBJECTS in

PNEUMATOLOGY, ETHICS,

AND

DIVINITY:

WITH

REFERENCES to the moſt conſiderable AUTHORS on each Subject.

By the late Reverend PHILIP DODDRIDGE, D.D.

The SECOND EDITION, Corrected.

LONDON,

Printed by Aſſignment from the Author's Widow,

For J. BUCKLAND, J. F. and C. RIVINGTON, W. CLARKE and R. COLLINS, S. CROWDER, T. LONGMAN, B. LAW, E. JOHNSTON, G. ROBINSON, R. BALDWIN, and W. OTRIDGE.

MDCCLXXVI.

THE
CARE of the SOUL
Urged as the
ONE THING NEEDFUL.

A
SERMON
PREACH'D
JUNE 22, 1735.

By P. DODDRIDGE, D.D.

Ὁ βυλόμενος ἀνθρώπυ ἐπιμελεῖθαι τῆς ψυχῆς ἐπιμελείσθω
τῆς λογικῆς.   Simplic.

The THIRD EDITION.

LONDON:
Printed for RICHARD HETT, at the *Bible* and
Crown in the *Poultry.* 1740.
[Price Four-Pence.]

THE
Scripture-Doctrine

OF

SALVATION by GRACE through FAITH,

Illuſtrated and improved in

Two SERMONS:

The Subſtance of which was Preached at

ROWELL in *Northamptonſhire*.

By P. DODDRIDGE, *D. D.*

Publiſhed, with ſome Enlargements, at the earneſt Requeſt of the Congregation there.

I am not aſhamed of the Goſpel of Chriſt ; for it is the Power of GOD *unto Salvation to every one that believeth.* Rom. i. 16.

LONDON:

Printed, and Sold by M FENNER, at the *Turk's-Head* in *Gracechurch-ſtreet* ; and JAMES HODGES, at the *Looking-glaſs* over-againſt *St. Magnus* Church, *London-bridge.* MDCCXLI.

[Price Eight-pence.]

THE RISE and PROGRESS OF RELIGION in the Soul:

ILLUSTRATED

In a COURSE of SERIOUS and PRACTICAL ADDRESSES,

Suited to PERSONS of every CHARACTER and CIRCUMSTANCE:

WITH

A Devout MEDITATION or PRAYER added to each CHAPTER.

By P. DODDRIDGE, *D. D.*

Quâ feret hic Greſſum, Fontes dabit arida Vallis,
 Inque cavas Foſſas depluet Agmen Aquæ:
Inſtaurabit Iter Vires; et Numinis Ora
 Viſurus Solymæ figet in Æde Pedem.
    Johnſt. Pſal. lxxxiv. 5, 6.

Teſtifying—— Repentance toward GOD, *and Faith toward our Lord Jeſus Chriſt.* Acts xx. 21.

Whom we preach, warning every Man, and teaching every Man in all Wiſdom; that we may preſent every Man perfect in Chriſt Jeſus. Col. i. 28.

The SIXTH EDITION.

LONDON:

Printed and Sold by J. WAUGH, at the *Turk's Head* in Lombard Street. MDCCL.

THE
FAMILY EXPOSITOR:
OR,
A PARAPHRASE AND VERSION
OF
THE NEW TESTAMENT;
WITH
CRITICAL NOTES,
AND
A PRACTICAL IMPROVEMENT OF EACH SECTION.
VOLUME THE FIRST;
CONTAINING THE FORMER PART OF
THE HISTORY OF OUR LORD JESUS CHRIST,
AS RECORDED BY
THE FOUR EVANGELISTS.
DISPOSED IN THE ORDER OF AN HARMONY.
By P. DODDRIDGE, D.D.
THE EIGHTH EDITION.
TO WHICH IS PREFIXED,
A LIFE OF THE AUTHOR,
BY
ANDREW KIPPIS, D.D. F.R.S. and S.A.

Ει δε τις υπο τινων μη πασχη των λογων, υπο μονων αν των εν αδυ δυκαςηριων υπευθυνθειη.   SIMPLIC. in EPICTET. Proem.

LONDON:
PRINTED BY H. BALDWIN AND SON,
FOR G. G. AND J. ROBINSON; R. BALDWIN; C. DILLY; F. AND C. RIVINGTON; J. MATHEWS; W. OTRIDGE AND SON; J. SCATCHERD; DARTON AND CO.; C. LAW; LONGMAN AND REES; J. WALKER; VERNOR AND HOOD; D. OGILVY AND SON; T. HURST; J. CUTHELL; LACKINGTON AND CO.; AND J. WALLIS.

MDCCXCIX.

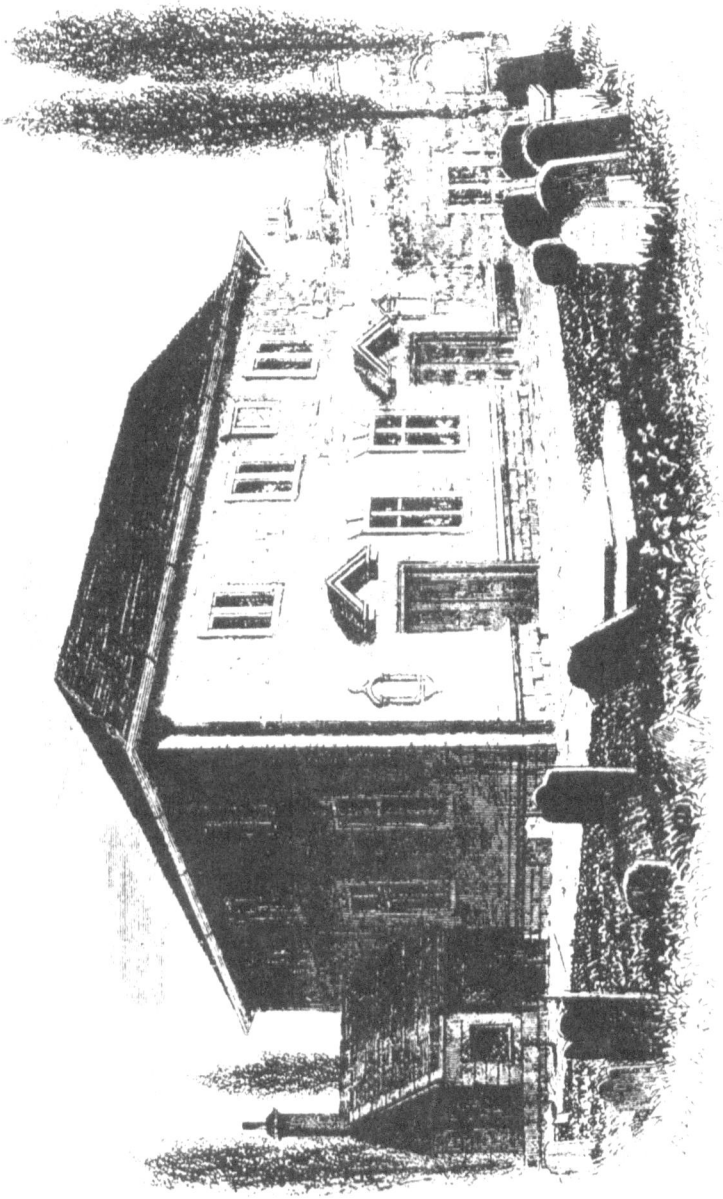

Castle Hill Meeting House, Northampton

The Northampton Academy

THE HOLY TRINITY

On so basic a doctrine as the Trinity, Doddridge honestly faced the problems we all have in making rational sense of our faith. He was afraid of giving the impression that there are three gods—a misunderstanding which the Athanasian creed might suggest—and equally he was at pains to avoid the idea that the names of the three persons are but mere names of *one* person—the Sabellian heresy. Following some intricate discussion, his statement of the Trinity in his *Divinity Lectures* is simple and straightforward:

> The Scripture represents the Divine being as appearing in, and manifesting himself by the distinct persons of *Father*, *Son*, and *Holy Ghost*, each of which has his peculiar province in accomplishing the work of our redemption and salvation, and to each of which we owe an unlimited veneration, love and obedience.[32]

The fundamental difficulty reason poses for faith is met by a quotation from Jeremy Taylor, the famous seventeenth century bishop:

> Dr Jeremiah Taylor says, 'that he who goes about to speak of the mystery of the trinity, and does it by words and names of man's invention, talking of essences and existences, hypostases and personalities, priorities in co-equalities, &c, and unity in pluralities, may amuse himself and build a tabernacle in his head, and talk something he knows not what; but the good man, that feels the power of the Father, And to whom the Son is become wisdom, sanctification and redemption, in whose heart the love of the Spirit of God is shed abroad, this man, though he understands nothing of what is unintelligible, yet he alone truly understands the Christian doctrine of the Trinity.'[33]

It is surely wise to settle the matter thus!

The early eighteenth century debates about the doctrine of the Trinity centred on the person of Christ. The most urgent question of the day was, 'What think ye of Christ; whose son is he?' Arianism denied the full deity of Christ, insisting that he was created rather than begotten, and, in his early years, Doddridge admits to leaning toward this view. By the time he commenced his ministry, his views were thoroughly orthodox. In the *Family Expositor* we read:

> (I AM ALPHA AND OMEGA). That these titles should be repeated so soon, in a connection which demonstrates they are given to Christ, will appear very remarkable. And I cannot forbear recording it, that *this text* has done more than any other in the Bible, toward preventing us from giving in to *that*

---

[32] *Works*, v. 187.
[33] Ibid. 193.

scheme, which would make our Lord Jesus Christ no more than a deified creature (*Note on Rev. 1:11*).³⁴

I am deeply sensible of the sublime and mysterious nature of the doctrine of Christ's deity, as here declared; but it would be quite foreign to my purpose to enter into a large discussion of that great foundation of our faith, it has often been done by much abler hands. It was, however, a matter of conscience with me, on the one hand, thus strongly to declare my belief of it; and, on the other, to leave it as far as I could in the simplicity of scripture expressions (*Note on John 1:1*).³⁵

Justly hath our Redeemer said, blessed is the man that is not offended in me: and we may peculiarly apply the words to that great and glorious doctrine of the *Deity of Christ*, which is here before us. A thousand high and curious thoughts will naturally arise in our corrupt hearts on this view of it; but may divine grace subdue them all to the obedience of an humble faith; so that, with Thomas, we may each of us fall down at his feet, and cry out with sincere and unreserved devotion, My Lord and my God! (*Comment on John 1:1–14*).³⁶

BIBLICAL CALVINIST

When such foundational truths of the Bible were discarded, it was common for many to preach a gospel of morality, rather than a gospel of Grace. When 'evangelical doctrines' were under threat, Doddridge made his unequivocal response in his two sermons on *Salvation by Grace*.

> Salvation by grace is not a subject which grows out of date in a few months. This glorious doctrine has been the joy of the church in all ages on earth; and it will be the song of all that have received it in truth throughout the ages of eternity, and be pursued in the heavenly regions with ever-growing admiration and delight.³⁷

At the very heart of the Gospel was the cross of our Lord Jesus Christ. For Doddridge, there was no salvation, but through the precious blood of Christ. It was a substitutionary atonement. In his impressive and moving sermon *Christ's Invitation to Thirsty Souls,* he declares:

> The tears of our blessed Redeemer must needs be convincing and affecting, if the mind be not sunk into an almost incredible stupidity; but his blood is still more so. View him, my brethren, not only in the previous scenes of his abasement, his descent from heaven, and his abode on earth; but view him on mount Calvary, extended on the cross, torn with thorns,

---

34 *Works*, x. 431.
35 *Works*, vi. 24.
36 Ibid. 29.
37 *Works*, ii. 553.

> wounded with nails, pierced with a spear; and then say, whether there be not a voice in each of these sacred wounds, which loudly proclaims the tenderness of his heart, and demonstrates, beyond all possibility of dispute or suspicion, his readiness to relieve the distressed soul, that cries to him for the blessings of the gospel. He died to purchase them, not for himself, but for us; and can it be thought he will be unwilling to bestow them? We may well conclude that he loved us, since he shed his blood to wash us from our sins (Rev. 1:5): For greater love hath no man than this, that a man lay down his life for his friends (John 15:13); but he hath commended his love toward us, hath set it off by this illustrious and surprising circumstance, that while we were strangers and enemies he hath died for us (Romans 5:8).[38]

That our salvation was in the hands of God, and that the initiative of redemption was with him, led Doddridge to embrace two other great Bible truths which were under attack in his day—Predestination and Election. In the *Family Expositor* we read:

> Let us go back with unutterable pleasure to the gracious purpose which he was pleased to form in his own compassionate breast, when he chose us in Christ before the foundation of the world, when he predestinated us through him to the adoption of children. Let us acknowledge the freedom of his grace in it, that we are thus predestinated according to the purpose of him who, with proper regard to the nature of his intelligent and free creatures, worketh all things agreeably to the good pleasure of his will, and maketh us accepted in the beloved, that we may be to the praise of the glory of his grace (*Comment on Eph. 1:1-14*).[39]

In short, grace was the saving work of a sovereign God. In his *Divinity Lectures* we read:

> From hence it will further appear, that the reason of God's predestinating some to everlasting life, was not fetched from a foresight of their faith and obedience, considered as independent upon any communication of grace from him, but that it is to be referred into his sovereign mercy and free grace; which is also the language of many other scriptures. Titus 3:4,5: Ephesians 2:8, 9.[40]

Therefore, as a concomitant to the natural unbelief of the human heart, Doddridge—with Calvin and Baxter—resolves the difference between the believer and unbeliever in terms of *Common* and *Special Grace*. In Christ's *Invitation to Thirsty Souls* he says:

---

38 Ibid. 601-2.
39 *Works*, ix. 328.
40 *Works*, v. 259.

I know, there is a great deal of difference between the common operations of the Spirit on the minds of those who continue obstinate and impenitent, and those special influences by which he sweetly but powerfully subdues the hearts of those, who are chosen in Christ Jesus before the foundation of the world. Yet I am persuaded, that none to whom the Gospel comes are utterly neglected by that sacred agent.[41]

As a theological tutor, Doddridge was aware of the danger of pushing logic too far: it must be kept under a tight rein. As with Richard Baxter before him, Doddridge resisted the temptation to deduce from election that Christ only died for the elect. There were too many 'alls' in Scripture. So, in his Divinity Lectures, Doddridge says:

> It is plain that there is a sense, in which Christ may be said to have died 'for all', i.e. as he has procured an offer of pardon to all, provided they sincerely embrace the Gospel. Cf. John 3:16, 6:50,51, Romans 5:18, 8:32, 1 Corinthians 8:11, 2 Corinthians 5:14,15,19, 1 Timothy 2:4, 6, Hebrews 2:9, 1 John 2:2.[42]

It is interesting to observe at this point, that Doddridge refers his students to John Calvin's views on the extent of the atonement. What Dr R. T. Kendall[43] stunned the Reformed Evangelical world with in 1979 was known to Baxter and Doddridge—that Calvin believed Christ died for all men.[44] The doctrine of limited atonement was an instance of logic going beyond Scripture. Thus Dr John Owen, whose view Baxter opposed, was called the 'over-orthodox doctor',[45] because of his work on the atonement, *The Death of Death in the Death of Christ* (1647). Owen's position was embryonic hyper-Calvinism—what Doddridge called 'High Calvinism'. He, like Baxter, was known as a 'moderate' (or 'true') Calvinist. For further discussion of these

---

41 *Works*, ii. 600.
42 *Works*, v. 214.
43 See *Calvin and English Calvinism* (Oxford: OUP, 1979), 13f.
44 Sample statements: Calvin on the extent of the Atonement:
   (a) It is incontestable that Christ came for the expiation of the sins of the whole world. Hence, we conclude that, though reconciliation is offered to all through him, yet the benefit is peculiar to the elect. God reconciles the world to himself, reaches to all, but that it is not sealed indiscriminately on the hearts of all to whom it comes so as to be effectual (*Concerning the Eternal Predestination of God*, tr. J. K. S. Reid (London: James Clarke, 1961), 148–9).
   (b) Paul makes grace common to all men, not because it in fact extends to all but because it is offered to all. Although Christ suffered for the sins of the world, and is offered by the goodness of God without distinction to all men, yet not all receive him (*Commentary on Romans* (5:18), tr. Ross Mackenzie (Edinburgh: Oliver & Boyd: 1961), 117–118).
   (c) Christ suffered sufficiently for the whole world but effectively only for the elect. I allow the truth of this (*Commentary on St John and 1 John*, (1 Jn 2:2) tr. T. H. L. Parker (Edinburgh: Oliver & Boyd, 1961), ii. 244).
45 See Nuttall, *Richard Baxter and Philip Doddridge*, 10.

and related issues I would refer the reader to my published doctoral thesis *Atonement and Justification* (1984)[46] and other more recent publications.

However, the efficacy of the atonement was guaranteed by election, and this was where 'moderate' Calvinism differed from the universalist view of the Arminians. So, with Baxter and Calvin, Doddridge the 'hypothetical universalist' says in his Lectures:

> There (is) a sense, in which Christ might be said to die for all; as all men partake of some benefit by his death, and such provision is made for their salvation, as lays the blame of their ruin, if they miscarry, entirely upon themselves: but it was in a very peculiar and much nobler sense, that he died for the elect, intending evidently to secure for them, and only for them, the everlasting blessings of his Gospel. John 10:15,16,26; 17:2,9,16.[47]

Doddridge had no inhibitions about being evangelistic as a result of the Bible's teaching about election. To say that God's sovereignty makes humans mere automatons, or that evangelism is unnecessary, and that strivings for holiness are pointless, is to abuse the doctrine of election and fly in the face of God's Word. Therefore, Doddridge shows us the biblical basis for human activity. In the *Family Expositor*, he says:

> (Will have all men to be saved) It is far from being my design, in any of these notes, to enter deep into controversy, but I must confess I have never been satisfied with that interpretation which explains all men here merely as signifying some of all sorts and ranks of men; since I fear it might also be said, on the principles of those who are fondest of this gloss that he also wills all men to be condemned. On the other hand, if many are not saved, it is certain the words must be taken with some limitation, which the following clause, he wills their coming to the knowledge of the truth, must also prove. The meaning therefore seems to be, that God has made sufficient provision for the salvation of all, and that it is to be considered as the general declaration of his will, that all who know the truth themselves, should publish it to all around them, so far as their influence can extend (*Note on 1 Tim. 2:4*).[48]

---

[46] See Alan C. Clifford, *Atonement and Justification: English Evangelicalism 1640-1790—An Evaluation* (Oxford: The Clarendon Press, 1990).

[47] *Works*, v. 263. For a more recent discussion of Doddridge's theology, see Richard A. Muller, 'Philip Doddridge and the Formulation of Calvinistic Theology in an Era of Rationalism and Deconfessionalization' in R. D. Cornwall and W. Gibson (eds.), *Religion, Politics and Dissent, 1660-1832* (Aldershot: Ashgate, 2010), 65-84. While he recognises the Baxter-Doddridge link, Dr Muller's attempt to distance Doddridge from Amyraut's type of hypothetical conditionalism is unfounded (see Doddridge, *Works*, v. 240; x. 327).

[48] *Works*, ix. 581.

THE HOLY SPIRIT

With the advent of the Methodist revival, attention became focused on the doctrine and work of the Holy Spirit. Doddridge made plain his view of the Holy Spirit's work in the new birth through his *Discourse on Regeneration*.[49] As regards what is known today as the 'Baptism in the Holy Spirit', Doddridge believed a distinction was to be drawn between the new birth and the baptism of the Spirit. In the *Family Expositor*, he comments on the outpouring of the Holy Spirit at Pentecost thus:

> Thus did the blessed Jesus accomplish what had been foretold concerning him (Matthew 3:11), that he should baptize his disciples with the Holy Ghost and with fire. And surely the sacred flame did not only illuminate their minds with celestial brightness, but did also cause their whole hearts to glow with love to God and zeal for his gospel. To this purpose, may he still be imparted to us, whether we hold public or private stations in the church; and may our regards to him be ever most dutifully maintained. Especially may he be poured out upon the ministers of it, to direct them how they should speak the wonderful things of God; and may their hearers, under his gracious energy, gladly receive the word (*Comment on Acts 2:1-21*).[50]

Doddridge understood the 'sealing' or 'witness' of the Holy Spirit in the context of the Pentecostal blessing. He expounds Romans 8:16 as 'some inward impression of God's Spirit upon the believer's mind, assuring them that they are Christians indeed'.[51] For this blessing Doddridge urges the doubting believer to 'Plead hard at the throne of grace. Lay hold on God by faith; and say, Lord, I will not let thee go till thou bless me.'[52] However, Doddridge also distinguished between the Baptism of the Spirit and the extraordinary gifts of the Spirit. Now that the Canon of Scripture was complete, the latter were not necessary. He was at one with the Reformers, Puritans and Methodists when he said that:

> Many things may be said of the charismata, or the extraordinary gifts and powers of the Apostles and primitive (early) Christians, which were so peculiar to that age, that we have no personal concern in them at all.[53]

MISSIONARY PIONEER

Doddridge also responded to the missionary challenge of the 'Great Commission' (Matt. 28: 18-20). It has to be said that missionary enterprise was slow to appear on the agenda of Protestants following the Reformation.

---

49 *Works*, ii. 371f.
50 *Works*, vii. 514.
51 *The Witness of the Spirit* in *Sermons* (London: J. Hatchard & Son, 1826), ii. 381.
52 Ibid. iii. 15.
53 *Works*, i. 554.

Even if Richard Baxter's enthusiastic support for John Eliot's mission to the American Indians was rare in the seventeenth century, Doddridge's similar passion for mission was not widespread in the early eighteenth century. With knowledge of the revival in New England (through reading Jonathan Edwards' *Narrative of Surprising Conversions*) and the success of David Brainerd among the Indians both serving to quicken Doddridge's zeal, he was to have a prophetic role in world mission besides a pioneering role in revival.

Sharing Baxter's zeal, Doddridge outlined his concerns for revival at an assembly of 'The Associated Protestant Dissenting Ministers in the Counties of Norfolk and Suffolk' held at Denton, Norfolk in June 1741. By all accounts, this was an extraordinary occasion. Doddridge's friend Richard Frost of Great Yarmouth wrote:

> A remarkable day indeed, when the presence of God filled our assembly; and not myself only, but many others have with pleasure owned it was one of the best days of our lives. Though the season was hot, the auditory very much crowded, and between four and five hours spent in public worship, none thought the hours tedious and wished for a dismission.[54]

Sadly, neither John Wesley nor George Whitefield had happy marriages, yet Doddridge could write thus to his beloved wife Mercy of this revival event:

> We spent Tuesday [June 30] at Denton & it was one of the most delightful days of my whole life. Seventeen ministers were there of whom 8 officiated indeed excellently well. We held a kind of council afterward concerning the methods to be taken for the revival of religion & I hope I have set them on work to some good purpose.[55]

Interestingly, while the Holy Spirit's presence was powerfully felt in a quiet and remote Norfolk village, the Journals of Wesley and Whitefield record nothing of much significance for 30 June 1741. Had J. C. Ryle not confined himself to Anglicans in his *Christian Leaders of the Last Century* (1885), he might have included this event, thus providing a fuller and inclusive picture of the wonderful work of God known as the Methodist Revival.

One scheme led to another. So, in October 1741, Doddridge preached a remarkable sermon at Kettering in Northamptonshire during another meeting of ministers. It was eventually published with the title *The Evil and Danger of Neglecting the Souls of Men*. John Stoughton, Doddridge's third biographer, is of the opinion that this work is worthy of a place alongside Baxter's *Reformed Pastor*, an 'incomparable treatise' according to Doddridge and so much admired by him. Indeed, both works continue to command the

---

54 *Good Doctor*, 179.
55 Ibid.

attention of the twenty-first century Church. Time taken in studying them today would be well spent.

When Doddridge published his Kettering sermon in 1742, he dedicated it to his brethren in Norfolk and Suffolk. The dedication included the proposals he advanced at Denton the previous June *plus* supplementary ones agreed at Kettering and among his own Northampton congregation. Concerned with 'the propagation of the kingdom of Christ in the world', it was proposed that 'petitions' be 'put up' to 'the throne of grace' for 'the advancement of the gospel in the world, and for the success of all the faithful servants of Christ, who are engaged in the work of it, especially among the heathen nations'.[56]

Here are suggestions, almost identical to those advanced by William Carey fifty years later, but made twenty years before Carey was born (1761)! It is quite possible that since Carey took Doddridge's *Family Expositor* with him to India, that he might have read and been stimulated by this moving sermon and set of proposals advanced by Doddridge. Is it possible that he discovered a copy in the Castle Hill vestry at the time of his baptism in Northampton in 1783? Dr Ernest Payne thought so:

> Had some stray copy of Doddridge's sermon on *The Evil and Danger of Neglecting the Souls of Men* come into Carey's hands? Or had its substance been mediated to him in some way? We do not know. But it is surely no coincidence that it was in Northamptonshire [Carey came from Paulersbury], in the Doddridge country and so nearly in the Doddridge manner, that the first of modern missionary societies [the Particular Baptist Mission] had its birth.[57]

PROTESTANT ECUMENIST

Doddridge shared Baxter's deeply-held passion for Christian Unity, what we would regard today as evangelical unity. He did all he could to root out bigotry and sectarianism, being a friend to all who 'Loved the Lord Jesus in sincerity and truth'. He was grieved at the Christian 'fragmentation' of his day. In his comment on John 17:21, he says:

> (That the world may believe that thou hast sent me.) This plainly intimates that dissentions among Christians would not only be uncomfortable to themselves, but would be the means of bringing the truth and excellence of the Christian religion into question: and he must be a stranger to what hath passed, and is daily passing, in the world, who does not see what fatal advantage they have given to infidels to misrepresent it as a calamity, rather than to regard it as a blessing to mankind. May we be so

---

56 Ibid. 180.
57 Ibid.

wise as to take the warning, before we are quite destroyed one of another! (Galatians 5:15) (*Note on John 17:21*).[58]

Doddridge was impatient with denominationalism, which he called 'party spirit'. He did all he could to bring Christian people together, believing that what was agreed upon was much greater than what divided them. Listen to his rebuke of our divisions:

> In the meanwhile, let us avoid, as much as possible, a party spirit, and not be fond of listing ourselves under the name of this, or that man, how wise, how good, how great so ever, for surely, if the names of Peter and Paul were in this view to be declined, much more are those, which, in these latter days, have so unhappily crumbled the Christian and Protestant interest, and have given such sad occasion to our enemies to reproach us. Christ is not divided: nor were Luther, or Calvin, or even Peter, or Paul, crucified for us; nor were we baptised into any of their names (*Comment on 1 Cor. 1:10-17*).[59]

Christian reunion did not mean the sinking of differences, or that our sincere convictions were to be suppressed. It was a case of 'speaking the truth in love', as he explained in a late sermon:

> Truth is indeed too sacred a thing ever to be denied on any consideration: and so far as we are in our own consciences persuaded that any particular truth is important, neither honour or charity will allow us to give it up, as a point of mere indifferent speculation. Let us therefore ever be ready, when properly called out to the service, to plead its cause in the name of the God of truth, but let it be in a manner worthy of him, a manner which may not offend him as the God of love. And let us be greatly upon our guard that we do not condemn our brethren, as having forfeited all title to the name of Christians, because their creeds or confessions of faith do not come up to the standard of our own.[60]

Doddridge possessed what was called a 'catholic' spirit. His concern for unity brought him a wide acquaintance. He had discussions with the Archbishop of Canterbury, Dr Herring, as well as Baptist Pastors; he was a friend of Methodist revivalists as well as more traditional Dissenters. However, it is obvious from his correspondence and writings that he was concerned with *Protestant* Unity, in days when no one doubted that the Church of England was a Protestant Church.

---

58 Note on John 17:21 (*The Family Expositor*), *Works*, vii. 339.
59 *The Family Expositor*, *Works*, viii. 564.
60 *Christian Candour and Unanimity* (1750), *Works*, iii. 267.

UNAMBIGUOUS PROTESTANT

If he could not justify perpetual divisions between the Protestant bodies, he had no doubts about the duty of separation from the Roman Catholic Church. In his sermon on the *Iniquity of Persecution*, he starts with this forthright statement:

> If Popery be considered in a religious view, it must appear the just object of our contempt, as well as our abhorrence.[61]

In another sermon, he explains his position very clearly:

> My brethren, pardon the freedom of my speech. I should have thought it my duty to have separated from the Church of Rome, had she pretended only to determine those things which Christ has left indifferent: How much more when she requires a compliance with those, which he hath expressly forbid? You shall not only bow at the venerable name of our common Lord, but you shall worship an image: You shall not only kneel at the communion, but kneel in adoration of a piece of bread: You shall not only pronounce, or at least appear to pronounce, those accursed, who do not believe what is acknowledged to be incomprehensible, but those who do not believe what is most contrary to our reason and senses. When these are the terms of our continued communion, the Lord judge between us and them! Had nothing but indifferent things been in dispute, we should have done, as we do by our brethren of the Church of England, taken our leave of them with decency and respect: We should have loved them as our brethren, while we could not have owned them as our Lords. But when they require us to purchase our peace, by violating our consciences and endangering our souls, it is no wonder that we escape as for our lives.[62]

For Doddridge, the position and power of the Pope, the doctrine of the Mass and transubstantiation, and worship of the Virgin Mary were major issues at stake. On papal power and influence, he says:

> (Above all that is called God, &c.) The usurpation of the papacy in Divine things is so unequalled, that if these words are not applicable to it, it is difficult to say, who there ever has been, or can be to whom they should belong. The manner in which the Pope has exalted himself above magistrates (civil governments) is equally remarkable and detestable (*Notes on 2 Thessalonians 2:4*).[63]
>
> The scandalous and extravagant pretences which the followers of the papacy have made to miracles, exceeding in number, and some of them in marvellous circumstances, those of Christ and his apostles, plainly

---
61 *Works*, iii. 119.
62 *Lectures on Popery*, quoted in 'Orton's Memoir', *Works*, i. 123.
63 *The Family Expositor*, *Works*, ix. 551

display the energy of Satan, that father of frauds, pious and impious. And the most incredible lies, which they have, by solemn and irrevocable acts, made essential to their faith, shew the strength of delusion (*Comment on 2 Thessalonians 2:1–12*).[64]

For Doddridge, the doctrine of transubstantiation was as ridiculous as it is unbiblical:

> (This is my body) When I consider that (as a thousand writers have observed) on the same foundation on which the papists argue for transubstantiation from these words, they might prove, from Ezekiel 5:1–5, that the prophet's hair was the city of Jerusalem; from John 10:9 and 15:1 that Christ was literally a door and a vine; and from Matthew 26:27,28, and from 1 Corinthians 11:25, that the cup was his blood, and that Christ commanded his disciples to drink and swallow the cup; I cannot but be astonished at the inference they would deduce from hence (*Note on Matt. 26:26*).[65]

Prayers to the Virgin Mary were a failure to grasp the nature of our Lord's authority as well as a denial of the direct access we have to the throne of grace:

> If his mother met with so just a rebuke for attempting to direct his ministrations in the days of his flesh, how absurd it is for any to address her as if she had a right to command him on the throne of his glory (*Comment on John 2:1–11*).[66]

It is plainly true, therefore, after the survey we have made of some of Doddridge's convictions, that he was far from indifferent to doctrine. Indeed, it was clearly of the greatest importance to him.

However, Doddridge also made it clear that there was more to being a Christian than doctrinal exactness and precision. He makes this judicious observation in the *Rise and Progress of Religion in the Soul*:

> The exercise of our rational faculties upon the evidences of divine revelation, and upon the declaration of it as contained in Scripture, may furnish a very wicked man with a well-digested body of orthodox divinity in his head, when not one single doctrine of it has ever reached his heart.[67]

Doddridge's views on Roman Catholicism may cause disappointment to some who have viewed him as an ecumenical prophet, and yet reassurance for others. It must be said in all truth that he clearly drew a distinction between Roman Catholicism and Roman Catholics, between the system

---
64 Ibid. 554.
65 Ibid. vii. 296.
66 Ibid. vi. 135.
67 *Works*, i. 422.

and its blind devotees. Nowhere is this more perfectly illustrated than in the 'Connell Affair'. One Bryan Connell was found guilty of murdering a man at Weedon, near Northampton. Doddridge befriended the poor man, who pleaded innocence, and Doddridge believed that he was not guilty. Despite an appeal, Connell was executed on 3 April 1741. Now Connell was a Roman Catholic, and Doddridge's concern for him even led many to suggest that the Reformed pastor had inclinations towards Roman Catholicism. In a letter to Connell, written only two days before the execution took place, Doddridge pleads with the condemned man to seek salvation in Christ. The letter also tells us a great deal about Doddridge—the Protestant, the Evangelical, the spiritual and truly Christian man that he was:

> I beseech you by the worth of your precious and immortal soul! that in these solemn moments, you guard against every false dependence. You well remember how frequently and how earnestly I have repeated this caution. I rejoice in finding you so often declare, that you put no confidence in the power of a Priest to forgive sin; nor in the efficacy of sacraments to save an impenitent sinner; nor in the intercession of saints and angels; nor in the value of your own blood, supposing it, in this respect innocent, to make satisfaction to God for the sins of your life; but that you desire to trust in the mercy of God, through the blood and intercession of our Lord Jesus Christ alone. Whatever your opinion of the Church of Rome may be, which this is not a time to debate, you are in all these things a very good Protestant in your notions; but let me remind you, Sir, that we cannot be saved by the soundest notions, but must feel their power to change our hearts, and must act upon them. I do therefore again, that I may deliver your soul and my own, solemnly exhort you most earnestly to seek the renewing influences of Divine grace, to change your sinful heart, and to fit you for the presence of God. Pray that God may give you repentance unto life, not merely a grief for temporal ruin, and a dread of that future punishment which the worst of men must desire to escape, but a repentance arising from the love of God, attended with a filial ingenuous (or sincere) sorrow for the indignity and dishonour which your sins have offered to so excellent and so gracious a Being. Oh! while there is yet hope fly to the blood and the righteousness of Christ, and to the free grace of God in the Gospel which is manifested to the greatest of sinners, and shall be manifested in you, if you sincerely believe. I am glad I have seen no crucifix near you, but in a spiritual sense to lie at the foot of the cross, and to look by faith unto him that died upon it, is the safest and best thing you can do. Pardon and grace, help and happiness must be sought here, not only by you, my friend, but by the most upright and virtuous man upon the earth, or he will appear a condemned sinner before

God. God is my witness that this is my refuge: let it be yours, and we may have a happier meeting than we have known upon earth.[68]

A GREAT MAN

For Doddridge, his Protestant, Reformed, and evangelical orthodoxy was no negative thing. For him, the truth of God should lead to the God of truth; the written word should lead us to the Incarnate Word, and Gospel of Christ should lead us to the Christ of the Gospel. Such was Doddridge's Christianity. Perhaps the verdict of earlier generations was not overstated after all. It was not for nothing that Doddridge's various activities as pastor, evangelist, academy tutor, author, philanthropist and patriot won him many admirers. The editors of the centenary edition of his complete *Works* (1802–5) claimed that Doddridge 'ranks with the brightest ornaments of the British nation, and of the Christian Church'. Praise was also international. After reading the Dutch translation of some of Doddridge's sermons, a pastor of the Reformed Church at Amsterdam, Wilhelmus Peiffers declared to the printer: 'Herewith I gratefully return you the work of Dr Doddridge, concerning the New Birth, Salvation by Grace, &c which I have read more than once with such uncommon pleasure, that I long to see all that excellent author has published. I did not know him by name; but from this incomparable masterpiece, in which the oratory of the ancients seems to be revived, he appears to be a very great man.'[69]

That said, the personal dynamic of his Christ-centred spiritual piety shone in all he did:

> Would to God that all the party-names, and unscriptural phrases and forms, which have divided the Christian world were forgot, and that we might agree to sit down together, as humble, loving disciples; at the feet of our common Master, to hear his word, to imbibe his spirit, and transcribe his life in our own.[70]

This was the main spring of Doddridge's Christianity—without which, it is impossible to arrive at a correct estimate of the man. He summed up the blessed secret of his life a secret all may share, in his own epigram on the family motto DUM VIVIMUS VIVAMUS (In living, LIVE), described by Dr Samuel Johnson as one of the finest in the English language:

> Live, while you live, the epicure would say,
> And seize the pleasures of the passing day,
> Live, while you live, the sacred preacher cries,

---

68 *Correspondence and Diary of Philip Doddridge, DD*, ed J. D. Humphreys (1829–30), iii. 556f; *Calendar*, ed. Nuttall, Letter 667). It seems that Connell was not converted (see Humphries, v. 425).
69 *Good Doctor*, 9.
70 Preface to *The Family Expositor, Works*, vi. 13.

> And give to God each moment as it flies.
> Lord, in my life let both united be,
> I live in pleasure, when I live to thee.[71]

POSTSCRIPT: THE HYMNS

Doddridge's spirit shone in his hymns. Since the scale of this present publication does not permit even a brief discussion of the hymns, for an extensive survey I direct the reader to the penultimate chapter of my biography.[72] However, to round this tribute off on a note of praise, appropriate for Doddridge's legacy, I cite a hymn not quoted there. Based on Psalm 40:16 (and when sung to Joseph Mainzer's (1801–51) majestic tune 'Mainzer'[73]), this example reveals the author's profound and joyful sense of the grandeur of the Gospel of God's grace:

> GOD of salvation, we adore
> Thy saving love, thy saving power;
> And to our utmost stretch of thought
> Hail the redemption thou hast wrought.
>
> 2. We love the stroke, that breaks our chain,
> The sword, by which our sins are slain;
> And, while abas'd in dust we bow,
> We sing the grace, that lays us low.
>
> 3. Perish each thought of human pride,
> Let God alone be magnified:
> His glory let the heavens resound,
> Shouted from earth's remotest bound.
>
> 4. Saints, who his full salvation know,
> Saints, who but taste it here below,
> Join every angel's voice to raise
> Continued, never-ending praise.[74]

SOLI DEO GLORIA

---

71 Nuttall, 'Doddridge's Life and Times', in *Doddridge and English Religion*, ed. Nuttall, 21 and other places.
72 *Good Doctor*, 193ff.
73 *Congregational Praise* (London: Independent Press, 1951), 14 and other hymn books.
74 *Hymns Founded on Various Texts of the Holy Scriptures*, Works, iii. 454–5.

BRIEF BIBLIOGRAPHY

For analysis, evaluation and comprehensive bibliographical information, see:

Clifford, A. C., 'Orthodoxy and the Enlightenment: Theology and Religious Experience in the Thought of Philip Doddridge, D.D. (1702–1751)' (M.Litt diss., University of Newcastle-upon-Tyne, 1977).

Strivens, R., *Philip Doddridge and the Shaping of Religious Dissent* (Farnham: Ashgate Publishing Limited, 2015).

By the same author

Alan C. Clifford, *Richard Baxter: The Gospel Truth* (Norwich: Charenton Reformed Publishing, 2016). ISBN 978-0-9929465-3-1, 457pp

The chief characteristic, and main strength, of the book is its combination of commitment with scholarly rigour in setting Baxter in a wider context than is usual. Reading it, one gets a rich sense of his intellectual and religious context, his 'networks' and 'afterlife' as we say nowadays, and not only that, but the other characters in the cast list receive a respectful attention such as they do not usually attract. Alan Clifford has managed to write a book about Baxter that is individual, original, persuasive and thought provoking, distinctively his, and that is a rare thing.
Neil Keeble, Emeritus Professor of English Studies, University of Stirling

Alan C. Clifford, *The Good Doctor: Philip Doddridge of Northampton—A Tercentenary Tribute* (Norwich: Charenton Reformed Publishing, 2002). ISBN 978-0-95267-163-3 320pp

The age of Wesley, Whitefield and Edwards was also the age of Philip Doddridge (1702-51). As a pastor, preacher, theologian, educator, author, hymn writer, philanthropist and patriot, he was a remarkable English Christian by any standard. His faithful, fragrant and far-reaching testimony to Christ made him unique in his day. This tribute introduces us to an attractive personality whose remarkable achievements merit renewed attention. At a time of confusion and uncertainty in church and society, the author believes that a rediscovery of Doddridge's contribution is long overdue.

REVIEW EXTRACTS

'A deeply interesting work about a fascinating Christian. ... the book is excellently presented, lavishly illustrated and good value for money' (*English Churchman*).

'Among other biographers ... Alan Clifford's book is now clearly indispensable. It is also warm, readable and challenging' (*News of Hymnody*).

'Lovers of Doddridge, Northampton, hymns, revival and the history of English Dissent, cannot afford to ignore this book' (*Evangelicals Now*).

Dr Clifford has ... done us a real service with the publication of his book in the 300th anniversary of Doddridge's birth. The book is well written and attractively produced. The narrative is interesting and informative' (*The Banner of Truth*).

'Doddridge's life and ministry are set out in a very readable way, and Dr Clifford's enthusiasm for his subject comes through on every page. ... [a] most valuable and stimulating tribute to one of the greatest stars in the Congregational firmament' (*Congregational Concern*).

'A scholarly and well presented book ... comprising a very useful appendix ... This book will make a valuable addition to any library and comes highly recommended' (*Our Inheritance*).

'[In] this enlightening biography ... our hearts warm to a man whose consuming desire was to win souls for Christ and whose strength and life were devoted to the glorifying of God' (*Peace & Truth*).

To Live is Christ by Richard Baxter with Introduction by Alan Clifford, Charenton Reformed Publishing, 2022 (ISBN: 978-099294-659-3, 151pp)

Many readers will be familiar with the better-known works of Baxter, such as *The Reformed Pastor* and *The Saints' Everlasting Rest*. Few will have come across many of his shorter tracts, including the two enclosed with this book, *Making Light of Christ* and *The Grand Question Resolved*. This is unfortunate, as Baxter's writing ministry breathes just as strongly through them. This ministry has lost little of its force with age. Rather, Baxter's pen bears so close an affinity with the apostolic writings themselves that there is an almost timeless quality to them. This has been appreciated by many generations of Christian readers and is now further extended for our sakes by Alan Clifford.

Clifford has written two absorbing biographical articles which accompany the Baxter tracts in the volume, one on Baxter himself and the other on Edmund Calamy III, Baxter's youthful admirer and posthumous publicist. The latter of these is an abridged version of material published last year by Hesed & Emet under the title *Calamy Celebrated* (see EC8099 for review). The former meanwhile affords illuminating insights, such as on Baxter's musings regarding global mission. Both articles contain Clifford's usual original-source references and helpful discussion.

Baxter's call to holiness of life is resounding and beguiling. Immersing oneself in Part II of The Grand Question, in particular, will stir any conscientious reader to self-examination of the most worthwhile variety. We can happily recommend this volume.

Edward Keene, *English Churchman*

Calamy Celebrated by Alan Clifford, H&E Publishing, 2022 (ISBN: 978-1-77484-022-1, 44pp)

This very welcome account of Edmund Calamy has Alan Clifford's characteristic clarity and forcefulness—that is, commitment—coupled with, again characteristically, an unrivalled familiarity with the primary sources. Its summary of the context and course of Calamy's life draws out clearly his character and significance, and accords this unduly neglected figure his true place and standing in the history of dissent. The rehabilitation of Calamy's Divine Mercy Exalted is especially persuasive. And all this is done with a liveliness and wit too rare in scholarly writing.

Neil Keeble, *Emeritus Professor of English Studies, University of Stirling*

JOHN JONES TALSARN, The People's Preacher by Alan C. Clifford, Charenton Reformed Publishing, 2013 (ISBN 978-0-9555165-8-0, 306 pp)

John Jones, Talsarn: The People's Preacher tells an important story. With encouragements for the dispirited believer on every page, Alan Clifford may have come along just in time to rescue the legacy of John Jones from undeserved oblivion. The appendices ... include a section on the preacher David Lloyd Jones, John's youngest son. Most appealing of all are the extracts from a 1907 Welsh biography of John's wife Fanny, deftly and sensitively rendered into English by Marian Clifford. Fanny's story, pulsing with humanity and not infrequently moving, merits a wide readership on its own account. This is the most heartfelt and enjoyable work I have read from this author. It is impossible not to be captivated by his love of his subject ... All preachers ought to buy this book, but no one will read it without spiritual profit.

David Llewellyn Jenkins

Alan C. Clifford, *Calvin Celebrated: The Genevan Reformer & His Huguenot Sons*, Charenton Reformed Publishing, 2009—commemorative new edition 2022 (ISBN: 978-095551-653-5, 168pp)

The English, to the extent that they are aware of the Reformation at all, are inevitably most familiar with its iteration on our own shores. Despite a valuable scholarly transition in recent decades to viewing the English Reformation in its wider European context, many of us remain relatively uninformed about any except the most prominent continental leaders. One such prominent leader is the eponymous Calvin. This book was first published to mark the great Frenchman's 500th birthday in 2009. This new edition came out last year to mark another significant, though darker anniversary—the 450th of the St Bartholomew's Day Massacre (an event exactly 90 years preceding our own 'Black Bartholomew').

As the subtitle indicates, this book is not just a Calvin biography—but a review also of five of his prominent successors in French Protestantism; Moise Amyraut (Professor and Pastor of Saumur, Anjou 1633-64), Jean Daillé (Pastor of Charenton, Paris 1626-70), Fulchan Rey (Itinerant preacher, 1685-86), Claude Brousson (Itinerant preacher, 1689-98), and Antoine Court (Head of the Lausanne Academy, 1729-60). These five span the period before and after the Revocation of the Edict of Nantes in 1685, a tragic turn in French religious policy which heralded the aggressive persecution of Protestants throughout the kingdom.

Clifford's writing is compelling and eminently readable. He strikes the right balance for a lay readership between depth and accessibility. Primary sources are well used but not overwhelming. The inherited landscape of relevant scholarship is navigated without its preoccupations distracting. An appropriate degree of familiarity with the historic environment is assumed. Most ordinary church members could benefit greatly from this work.

The testimony of any faithful church under fire is remarkable, not least the Huguenots of France. Clifford movingly relates their 'desert assemblies' in caves and forest clearings and the courage which they showed for the sake of Christ in the face of murderous threats. Variation of tone is provided as Clifford defends some of his subjects from historic accusations of coldness or severity, noting by turns the enjoyment of games, the tenderness of marriages, and kindnesses toward children. Likewise, some of the unjust criticisms levelled at 'Calvinism' are debunked.

Despite the proximity of France, the successes and sufferings of its church are a narrative which we know too little. Thanks are due to the author of this book in bringing some remedy here.

Edward Keene, *English Churchman*

About the author

Dr Alan Clifford (b. 1941) hails from Farnborough, Hampshire. Reared in Methodism and converted in Anglicanism (1958), he embraced Puritanism through the influence of Dr D. Martyn Lloyd-Jones (1963). An engineering career at the Royal Aircraft Establishment and the RAF Institute of Aviation Medicine, Farnborough (1958–66) was terminated after God's call to pastoral ministry. This led to university study (University of Wales, Bangor, 1966–69) and eventual ordination to the Congregational ministry (1969). He remains (since 1988) a minister without-charge of the Presbyterian Church of Wales. Now retired, Alan pursued pastoral ministry in Northampton, Gateshead, Great Ellingham, Norfolk, and Norwich. Academic profile: BA (philosophy) 1969; MLitt (philosophy of religion) 1978; PhD (historical theology) 1983. An in-depth study of Arminianism and Calvinism, Dr Clifford's doctoral thesis was published by Oxford University Press in 1990. Author of several books (and a few hymns) on this and related themes include Philip Doddridge and Welsh Calvinistic Methodism. Richard Baxter and Dr Edmund Calamy have occupied his attention in recent years.

CENTER *for* BAPTIST STUDIES
at THE SOUTHERN BAPTIST THEOLOGICAL SEMINARY

The Andrew Fuller Center for Baptist Studies, located at The Southern Baptist Theological Seminary in Louisville, Kentucky, seeks to promote the study of Baptist history as well as theological reflection on the contemporary significance of that history. The center is named in honor of Andrew Fuller (1754–1815), the late eighteenth- and early nineteenth-century English Baptist pastor and theologian, who played a key role in opposing aberrant thought in his day as well as being instrumental in the founding and early years of the Baptist Missionary Society. Fuller was a close friend and theological mentor of William Carey, one of the pioneers of that society.

The Andrew Fuller Center holds an annual two-day conference in September that examines various aspects of Baptist history and thought. It also supports the publication of the critical edition of the Works of Andrew Fuller, and from time to time, other works in Baptist history. The Center seeks to play a role in the mentoring of junior scholars interested in studying Baptist history.

andrewfullercenter.org

H&E Publishing is a Canadian evangelical publishing company located out of Peterborough, Ontario. We exist to provide Christ-exalting, Gospel-centred, and Bible-saturated content aimed to show God to be as glorious and worthy as He truly is.
hesedandemet.com

www.ingramcontent.com/pod-product-compliance
Lightning Source LLC
Chambersburg PA
CBHW021126080526
44587CB00010B/647